D0551454

Cat
Yoga

CAT YOGA

An Hachette UK Company
www.hachette.co.uk

Summersdale Publishers Ltd
Part of Octopus Publishing Group Limited
Carmelite House
50 Victoria Embankment
LONDON
EC4Y 0DZ
UK

www.summersdale.com

Printed and bound in China

ISBN: 978-1-78783-246-6

Substantial discounts on bulk quantities of Summersdale books are available to corporations, professional associations and other organizations. For details contact general enquiries: telephone: +44 (0) 1243 771107 or email: enquiries@summersdale.com.

Cat Yoga

OKAY, I'M READY FOR
THAT SWEET ZEN NOW...

Dannyboy
and Sam Hart

summersdale

AM I DOING IT YET?

I CALL THIS
"SUN SALUTATION VARIATION 45".

MICE COME AND GO LIKE
CLOUDS DRIFTING ON THE BREEZE...
I DO NOT NEED TO CHASE THEM ALL...

WHAT I THINK I LOOK LIKE
DOING EAGLE POSE
VS
WHAT I ACTUALLY LOOK LIKE
DOING EAGLE POSE...

I CAN MAKE ANY KIND
OF YOGA *HOT YOGA.*

THIS POSE REALLY HELPS
ME RELEASE ALL MY TOXIC ENERGY.

OOPS, LOOKS LIKE I MISSED A SPOT
IN MY LAST GROOMING SESSION...

OF COURSE I'M NOT JUST IN IT
FOR THE SHAVASANA...

I CALL THIS POSE
"EXTENDED HAIRBALL BEND".

I THOUGHT YOU SAID
THIS WAS MEANT TO BE
A RESTING POSE?

MY BODY IS A TEMPLE.

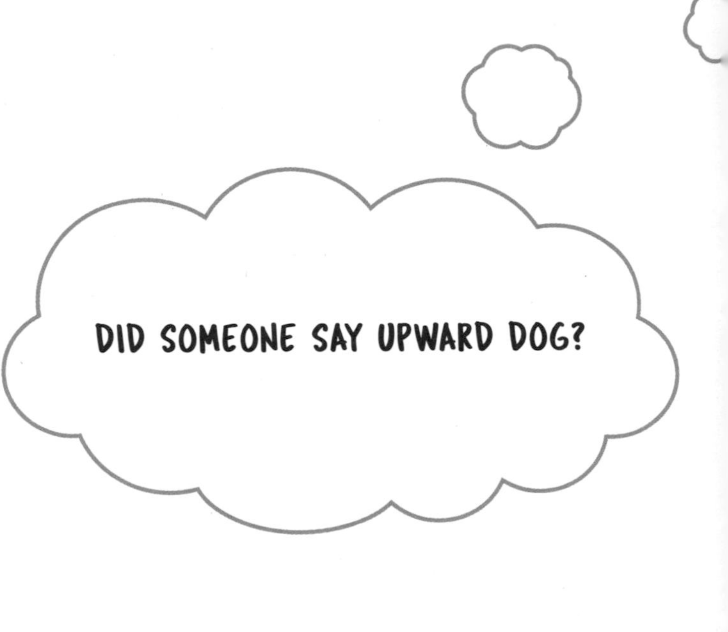
DID SOMEONE SAY UPWARD DOG?

OOH, GREAT CAT POSE!

REALLY GOOD AT YOGA?
OR JUST TOO MUCH CATNIP?

NOW I'LL ENTER WARRIOR POSE...

THE LIGHT IN ME *REALLY* WANTS
TO HONOUR THAT TUNA SANDWICH.

NOPE, DIDN'T HELP.
I STILL WANT TO PICK A FIGHT
WITH FELIX FROM NEXT DOOR.

BOOM! KEYBOARD WARRIOR POSE.

YOGA HAS MADE ME SO FLEXIBLE...

WHAT? HE'S JUST
PRACTISING CORPSE POSE.

YOGA HELPED ME FIND THE LIGHT.

TIME FOR MY FAVOURITE:
PIGEON POSE.

TODAY I'M GOING TO FOCUS
ON MY YOGIC BREATHING.
OUT THROUGH THE LEFT NOSTRIL...

THIS IS WHAT YOGA MATS ARE FOR, RIGHT?

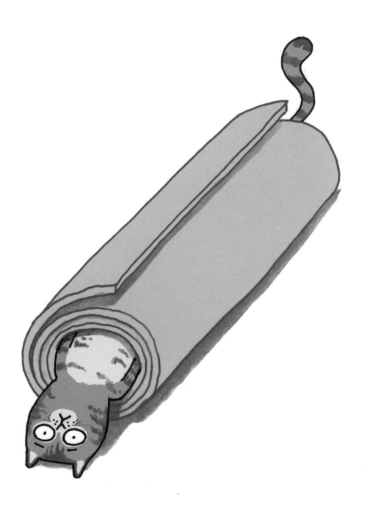

MEDITATING: DO NOT INTERRUPT.

I LIKE TO DO FIVE SUN SALUTATIONS
EVERY MORNING BEFORE MY
THIRD NAP OF THE DAY.

WELCOME TO MY YOGA STUDIO.

DISAPPOINTED: I THOUGHT CROW POSE
WOULD BE MUCH MORE FUN THAN THIS.

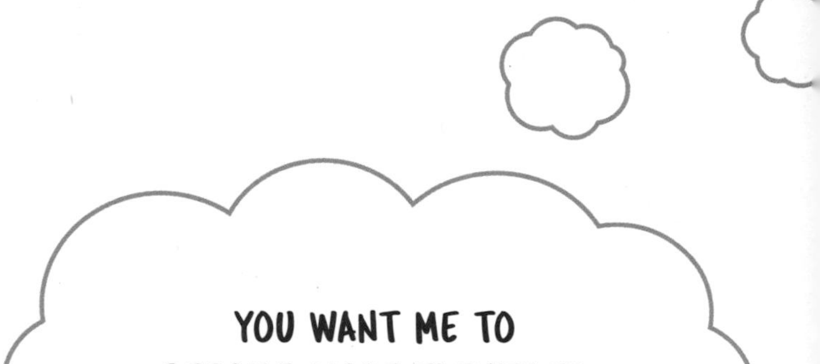
YOU WANT ME TO BECOME MORE FLEXIBLE?

HOW AM I EXPECTED TO BE ZEN
SURROUNDED BY ALL THIS CLUTTER?

YOGA GIVES ME TIME TO PAWS
AND REFLECT... OMMM-EOW...

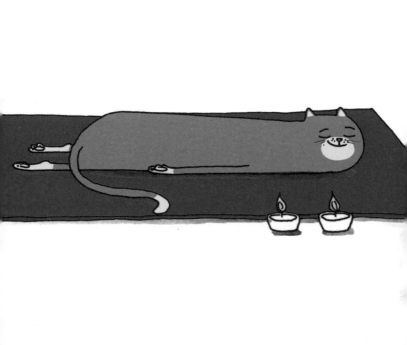

PERFECTING MY TREE POSE.

WHAT? LIKE YOGA IS HARD?

SHAVASANA? MORE LIKE SHAVASA-NAP.

NOBODY SAID SHOULDER STANDS
HAD TO INVOLVE GOING UPSIDE DOWN.

SO THIS ISN'T FISH POSE?

THE CAT SAT ON THE MAT...
AND DID YOGA... IN A TOGA.

MEDITATION IS REALLY IMPORTANT TO ME...
SINCE I'M NOT ALLOWED TO SCRATCH
PEOPLE WHO ANNOY ME ANY MORE...

OKAY, I'M READY FOR
THAT SWEET ZEN NOW...

If you're interested in finding out more about our books,
find us on Facebook at **Summersdale Publishers**
and follow us on Twitter at **@Summersdale**.

www.summersdale.com